THE FUTURE
OF
BUDDHISM

THE FUTURE
OF
BUDDHISM
and Other Essays

Sogyal Rinpoche

RIDER

LONDON • SYDNEY • AUCKLAND • JOHANNESBURG

1 3 5 7 9 10 8 6 4 2

First published in France in 2000, under the title *L'Avenir du bouddhisme*, by The Tertön Sogyal Trust

This edition first published in 2002 by Rider, an imprint of Ebury Press, Random House, 20 Vauxhall Bridge Road, London SW1V 2SA

Random House Australia (Pty) Limited
20 Alfred Street, Milsons Point, Sydney,
New South Wales 2061, Australia

Random House New Zealand Limited
18 Poland Road, Glenfield,
Auckland 10, New Zealand

Random House South Africa (Pty) Limited
Endulini, 5A Jubilee Road,
Parktown 2193, South Africa

The Random House Group Limited Reg. No. 954009

Papers used by Rider are natural, recyclable products made from wood grown in sustainable forests.

Printed and bound by
Biddles Ltd, Guildford and King's Lynn

A CIP catalogue record for this book
is available from the British Library

ISBN 0-7126-1564-4

Contents

Introduction

The four teachings that comprise this book spring from Sogyal Rinpoche's twenty-five years' experience of teaching Buddhism in the West. The two conference addresses and two articles presented here cover a wide range of topics. These include the issues facing Buddhism as it takes root in the modern world, an exploration of the healing power of the mind and guidance for anyone trying to follow a spiritual path today.

We begin with 'The Future of Buddhism', a keynote address that Rinpoche was invited to give for the audience of Buddhist practitioners, teachers and scholars at the 'Buddhism in America' conference in San Diego, California in May 1998. In November of the same year, the first International Congress for Tibetan Medicine was held in Washington DC. Opened by His Holiness the Dalai Lama, this unique gathering brought together Tibetan physicians, Lamas, doctors and medical specialists from many countries. On its first morning, Sogyal Rinpoche addressed the conference on 'The Spiritual Heart of Tibetan Medicine: Its Contribution to the Modern World'.

The two articles that follow were written specially by Rinpoche for *View* magazine. In the first of these, 'View and Wrong View', he offers advice on how to see through doubt and suspicion, and how to recognise wrong views for what they are. Finally, in 'Misunderstandings', Rinpoche reflects on how important it is to see through the mind and its delusions, while on the spiritual path, and to find confidence and strength in our own true nature.

1

The Future of Buddhism

*Speaking on the future of Buddhism, all I can do today is
to offer some thoughts and aspirations based on my own
experience and observations while teaching in the West over
the past twenty-five years. What I say will inevitably have
much to do with the Buddhist tradition of Tibet, and yet
I hope that it will hold some interest or meaning for
practitioners of any tradition.*

*I hasten to point out, to begin with, that I am just a
practitioner, doing my best to practise, simply a student of the
Dharma, who is trying, by working with myself, with the help
of the teachings and my masters, to become a better human
being. Let me say how honoured I am to be invited to address
this conference on Buddhism in America.*

I

Thinking about the Buddhadharma and its future, my
mind turns to my master Jamyang Khyentse Chökyi

❦ 3 ❦

Lodrö, who was a master of all the lineages of Tibetan Buddhism and who passed away in exile in Sikkim in 1959. He was truly a leader, regarded by many as one of the greatest Tibetan masters of the twentieth century, the embodiment of Tibetan Buddhism and living proof of what someone who had realised the teachings would be. He was a master of masters, the teacher of many of the great Lamas who were to teach in the West, such as Dilgo Khyentse Rinpoche, Kalu Rinpoche and Dezhung Rinpoche, yet he treated everyone equally, rich or poor, high or low.

I often wonder whether the whole future of Tibetan Buddhism might not have been different had he lived longer, to inspire its growth in exile and in the West with the same authority and infinite respect for all traditions that had made him so beloved in Tibet.

Jamyang Khyentse had a vision. He was, in fact, the heir to the non-sectarian Rimé movement which had swept through the eastern part of Tibet during the nineteenth century. This was a kind of spiritual renaissance which rejected all forms of sectarian, partisan bias and encouraged each tradition to master completely the authentic teachings and practice of its own lineage, while at the same time maintaining a spirit of openness, harmony and co-operation with other Buddhist schools. There was no blurring or synthesis of one tradition with another – the purity of each was ensured – but they co-existed and often drew inspiration from one another.

I see an intriguing parallel between the extraordinary richness of the spiritual culture of Tibet at the time of the great pioneers of this Rimé movement, such as Jamyang Khyentse Wangpo and Jamgön Kongbrul, and the great variety of lineages we find in the West today. In some ways the Rimé vision offers a model of how the Dharma must continue in the West and in America: with total respect for our separate authentic traditions and yet with an eye to the creativity and resourcefulness of different branches of Buddhadharma as they have settled into the American landscape. We can all inspire, help and network with one another, yet without confusion or inappropriate mixing of our traditions.

Jamyang Khyentse also saw that the Dharma would come to the West. In Tibet there had been many prophecies, from the time of Padmasambhava onwards, that this would occur, and Jamyang Khyentse spoke of it a number of times. He told the Tibetan master Tulku Urgyen in Sikkim not long before he passed away: 'From now on, the Buddhadharma will spread further, in the West.'

Looking now at the sheer impact that the Dharma has already had on the mainstream of Western life, one can only marvel at the number of different areas of American culture which have been touched by Buddhist influence, and which are very familiar now to us all:

❀ serving the dying and hospice care; a field very close to my own heart;

- ✿ mind/body medicine and healing;
- ✿ the world of psychology and therapy;
- ✿ the arts and education – we only have to think of the Naropa Institute;
- ✿ interfaith dialogue and ecumenical exchange;
- ✿ the life sciences;
- ✿ movements for peace and non-violence;
- ✿ right livelihood and ethics in business;
- ✿ ecology and green issues
- ✿ and, not to forget, in the case of Tibetan Buddhism, Hollywood and the movie industry!

The various Buddhist lineages have established themselves in one way or another in America, and many wonderful expressions of Buddhist-inspired action have emerged under the banner of Engaged Buddhism. I think of Glassman Roshi's Greyston Mandala, the Zen Hospice Project, the various initiatives in prisons, the work of Thich Nhat Hanh, and the Buddhist Peace Fellowship. I would like to celebrate them all, and I know how much Jamyang Khyentse – and all the masters of the Rimé tradition, if they were here – would have appreciated and applauded them.

Two Ways to Present the Dharma

In recent times His Holiness the Dalai Lama has been pointing out that there are two ways to present the Dharma today. One is to offer the teachings, in the spirit of Buddhism, without any notion of exclusivity or conversion, but as openly and as widely as possible, to be of service to people everywhere, of any background or faith. Since the heart of the Buddhadharma, the essential View, is so very practical, simple and yet profound, it can enrich and deepen anyone's understanding, regardless of what spiritual path he or she might follow.

The second way is to present the teachings for those who have a serious wish to follow the Dharma so that they can pursue a complete and thorough path, in whichever tradition.

What is the relationship between these two ways of teaching? The first cannot happen without the second. We must never forget that the uniqueness and great strength of the Dharma is that it is a *complete* spiritual path, with a pure, living lineage, unbroken to this day, and if we lose that, we have lost everything.

I see the Dalai Lama's statement as a blueprint for us all in the twenty-first century, and crucial for the survival of authentic Buddhism.

Some Concerns

How will Buddhism in the future find the way to make its fullest contribution towards the transformation of society? And yet how can we avoid it being absorbed and neutralised by its encounter with the contemporary world, so that it is reduced to yet another tool with which to numb us, conscripted and 'integrated' into Western society, to become simply an interesting offshoot of psychology, a branch of the New Age or part of the alternative health movement? Many of the Tibetan masters I know today have the same concerns and are asking themselves the same questions as Western Buddhists as we pass through this period of transition together. They also have concerns of their own. They see a number of warning signs for the future.

When we see Buddhist images on advertising hoardings, in Hollywood films and as icons of the chic, it *is* a testimony to the popularity of Buddhism. This can be gratifying, even exhilarating – but at the same time chilling. Because where will the popularity of Buddhism lead? Are we witnessing the conversion of Buddhism into a product, something which is quick and easy to master and which ignores the patient discipline and application that is really needed on the Buddhist path, as on any other spiritual path? In trying to make Buddhism palatable to American tastes and fashions, are we subtly editing or rewriting the teachings of Buddha? Is there a risk of Buddhism being 'sold' too hard, and being too pushy, even evangelical? Commercial-style grasping seems foreign to Buddhism, where the emphasis has always been on examining ourselves. Driven by our compulsive desire for something 'new', what will be the long-term result of seeking to put a little bit of knowledge into action too soon: rushing in too early, merely in order to be productive? My feeling, and that of the masters I know, is that practicality should never take priority over the authenticity of the teachings.

Understanding and Change

Whatever our concerns about the manner in which Dharma is presented, as far as the future is concerned, the overriding need is for us to deepen our *understanding* and *experience* of the Dharma.

Take the issue of making changes and adaptation, for example. It is time now, I feel, to present the *essence* of the teachings, without cultural paraphernalia, and yet without compromising the force or edge of the Dharma, while at the same time offering something appropriate for the conditions and mentality of modern Western people. This is the challenge. Not to remain too rigidly traditional but to adapt in an authentic manner; neither to hurry too much nor to wait too long, but to strike a middle way.

Of course, it is easy enough to adapt and make changes, but in my case what has always held me back has been the need I have felt to be absolutely certain that the result will be *truly* Dharma, in every way. For once we create a form, the tendency is for the form to stick, and then prove very difficult to change.

In Tibet, 1,200 years ago when the teachings of Indian Buddhism were being transplanted, there were exceptional Indian masters and Tibetan translators present to inspire the full integration of the teachings in a Tibetan setting, and to strike the right balance between maintaining the integrity of the teachings and channelling them into the bedrock of Tibetan culture and the Tibetan psyche. I sometimes wonder whether we today have the same qualities as they did.

Even the title 'translator' (*lotsawa*) had a much deeper significance then than it does now. It was a term of great respect, implying a profound understanding; Milarepa's master Marpa, for example, was called 'Marpa the translator'. This is what we need too – authentic scholars, like those Indian panditas and great Tibetan translators, who have the discernment, in making the translation to create an appropriate form without *ever* losing the essence. To put it simply: to make changes we need an extremely clear understanding of the teachings; it's a question of a very subtle, profound translation.

Suppose, for example, we alight upon some aspects of the teachings which seem inconvenient and we assume they are cultural paraphernalia. How can we be sure we are not making a huge mistake and dismissing what might in fact be an integral part of the teaching? We talk of cultural paraphernalia from the East, but in approaching the Buddhadharma, we of course bring with us the cultural preconceptions of the West, which may be even harder to identify or dissolve.

His Holiness the Dalai Lama has observed that there *are* aspects of the tradition which are due to geography, time and culture and which will change as conditions differ; but there are many other aspects which are a compassionate, skilful manifestation of wisdom based on an inherent truth. So when things become complex and difficult, we must take extra care not to throw out the baby with the bathwater.

Not that I advocate simply preserving some 'old tradition'. In my heart of hearts it has always been my deepest wish to find ways to transmit the Dharma for the present-day world, and it has been, and remains, a constant process of learning: from my teachers, from the teachings and from my own students.

However, one thing I have observed is that when, through study, practice and integration, a student of the Dharma does arrive at real and full understanding, then they become a *vessel* for the Dharma, and they begin to have the 'wisdom of discernment'. I pray that this wisdom of discernment may grow among practitioners of the Dharma and their understanding will become so complete that when adaptations are made, they will quite naturally be appropriate. So, even an essential presentation or a simple explanation of the teachings we make *now* must not in future turn out to have put limits on understanding or impeded the fullness of the Dharma. Wisdom, insight, experience, realisation – all of these we need, and especially skilful means.

At any rate, the challenge of our time is to steer a course between the standards of tradition and the perceived demands of a new situation. This is no easy task, and it is a dangerous and precarious one. Decisions we take now could have very far-reaching consequences in the future. And yet we must meet this challenge, striking a fine balance between creative daring and sober caution, but at the right pace, as the Dalai Lama has advised, and with the right understanding.

Whenever I consider introducing some important change, I *always* consult my masters, to be sure of avoiding the pitfall of merely putting 'my' seal on the teaching.

I I

In my mind, for the years to come, the issues of paramount importance will be: the thoroughness of training; the authenticity of the Dharma in both teaching and practice; and the support of the Sangha. In a way they evoke, respectively, the principles of Buddha, Dharma and Sangha.

Training

Buddhadharma is in the West, and it is not the preserve or monopoly of any Asian group. There is a saying in Tibetan: 'The Dharma is no one's property; it belongs to whoever has the true knowledge.' Westerners are, will be, and must be holders of these traditions, yet it is not simply an issue of authorisation, but one of *training*, or education. I know that many masters in the Tibetan tradition are concerned over the present quality of training these days. They say that a monk venerated today as a doctor of philosophy in the exile community in India can in fact be far less well trained than someone following the same studies in Tibet in the past. If this is the case in India, they ask, then what does it say about the standard of training in the West?

The great question is how, in today's turbulent, fast-paced and restless world, students can find ways to train in and practise the teachings with the calm and steady *consistency* necessary to realise their truth. In the past, people stayed in one place and followed a master almost all their lives – look at Milarepa, serving Marpa for years before he left him to practise on his own, or in our time the great Dilgo Khyentse Rinpoche, who served and stayed by my master Jamyang Khyentse for years. It requires a continuous transmission, and there is no substitute or alternative to consistency and stability.

Even in my own work I have seen how, when students devote themselves to training the mind and working with themselves over time, and in a special environment, they can achieve remarkable results.

From the traditional point of view, the training is tailored to whether a person wants to become a practitioner, a scholar or a teacher, but all three require a solid grounding in the basic Dharma teaching. The main points, the heart of the teaching, must be instilled in the student's mind so that he or she will never forget them. For example: refraining from harm, the crux of the Fundamental Vehicle; developing Good Heart, the essence of the Mahayana; and Pure Perception, the heart of the Vajrayana.

Equally there must be a good grounding in:

❀ meditation practice
❀ training in compassion
❀ understanding the nature of mind

In my work over the years I have discovered how important it is for students to establish this basis in the Dharma, and really come to some inner understanding, in the right kind of environment. This they need to return to again and again, whilst at the same time continuing, with different kinds of support, to follow a graduated path of study and practice, on which they accomplish as much as they can at the level they are on.

The most appropriate approach, I feel, is the Mengak Nyongtri Chenpo, the method of Patrul Rinpoche, from the Dzogchen lineage, where the master applies the training to the experience of the student. The traditional requirements of the practice can, in some ways, be adapted to the student's experience.

To pass on the teachings of Buddha is a tremendous responsibility and demands us always to examine our own *motivation*. One of my teachers, Nyoshul Khen Rinpoche, told me someone once asked him: 'What are the qualities needed to be a Dharma teacher?' He replied: 'To have a pure motivation.' The prime concern of Tibetan masters will always be that (1) the source of the transmission is *pure*, and (2) the motivation to teach is *pure* – the bodhisattva ideal. The key qualities in a Dharma practitioner that a teacher will always look for, with an eye to the continuity of the lineage, are (1) that he or she is a *good* human being: reliable, genuine, with their basic character and being tamed by the Dharma teaching itself, and (2) that their motivation is one of bodhicitta. The Dalai Lama has warned: 'Too many people have the Dharma only on their lips. Instead of using the Dharma to destroy their own negative thoughts, they regard the Dharma as a possession and themselves as the owner.' At all costs, a teacher must avoid failing the Buddhadharma with his or her own limitations, ego and personal agenda.

The Teachings

Another task, also of crucial importance, will be to sustain the integrity of what is called in Tibetan the 'Shedrup kyi Tenpa', the teaching of study and practice. They must always go hand in hand. Many Tibetan teachers are concerned at how individuals are studying in a piecemeal fashion, rather than following a complete path going through the major Buddhist texts. Studying the Dharma is essential, and yet the goal is not simply learning for its own sake: study must always be married to practice. The Dalai Lama has written: 'Buddhism places great importance on inner investigation, on training to develop the mind. From a Buddhist point of view, teaching and studying the Dharma is not merely an academic pursuit. We study and teach the Dharma in order to discipline our unruly minds.'

This tradition has produced the most amazing *practising scholars*, who have gone deeply into the experience of the practice of the teachings. I think of His Holiness the Dalai Lama again as a prime example. When it comes to the study and practice of the Dharma, its depth, wisdom and skilful means must not be compromised, otherwise in the future we might end up with a Buddhism which is not based on the teaching of Buddha. And in a society with no spiritual culture or the discernment it provides, people are gullible and so will be unable to determine what is genuine Buddhism, and what is not.

There are two special issues which I believe are of fundamental significance for the future: the need to cultivate a much deeper *appreciation* of the teachings and what they really offer and represent; and the attention that must be given to how true *integration* of the teachings takes place in the student's mind and heart.

APPRECIATION

I am constantly amazed to see how transforming the teachings can be, and how therapeutic. More and more I have realised the extent to which the teachings contain answers that we are often blind to; but when they are fully explored and experienced, and directed to the heart of a problem or delusion, it can have extraordinary effects. I feel that often we are not truly exploring the teachings themselves for what they contain, or letting them speak to the heart of the real difficulties that people, and Dharma practitioners, live with today.

For many years my whole attention has been drawn towards such questions as: How can people inspire and sustain themselves on their spiritual path? In what way can they make the most of their understanding and realisation? How can we truly apply the teachings to ourselves and the difficulties we face?

I recently spent one month in retreat with a group of students in our retreat centre and community in France. There we went deeply into the teachings, looking at the basic teachings but from the highest point of view, exploring their meaning together in quiet contemplation and reflection, and I marvelled at the kind of realisation and leaps in understanding that, even in so short a span of time, individuals went through. It brought it home to me that, in such a special environment, students can make discoveries about themselves which will stay with them for a long time, casting light into corners of darkness, really changing the way they see themselves and giving them a new ability to overcome the challenges life throws at them and the obstacles that arise in their own minds. I found this intensely moving and I pay homage to their understanding, courage and wholehearted dedication.

For example, one person said he suddenly began to see through the ploys of ego, and unmask delusion for what it was – masquerading behind the everyday moods and humdrum frustration which were screening him from the Dharma and robbing him of the chance to change. Someone else hit upon a method for skilfully outwitting one of the traps that ego habitually set for her. Several individuals reached a point where they realised and committed themselves, as never before, to taking responsibility for the training of their own minds. One Dharma practitioner of some years' standing saw through a habitual notion that had subtly dogged her for years – that happiness existed outside of herself and 'somewhere else'. She went on to discover in the Dharma a tremendous source of fulfilment, inner contentment and nourishment; she realised that until we can find the happiness and joy of Dharma, it is difficult to renounce samsara fully, and true renunciation is far from being bleak, joyless and cold hearted.

Different aspects of the teaching – meditation, reflection, love and compassion or visualisation – when explored with depth and inspiration, all have their ways of addressing the 'difficult' parts of ourselves, helping us to dissolve the masks and personas we hide behind. Some shift which may appear extremely simple can have a momentous effect on a person's life: the decision simply to be happy, or to leave behind or burn away some story from the past.

In such moments, students can empower themselves to cut through their attachments to samsara and its secret hiding places. They can recognise that the delusion and suffering which has been locked into their hearts and minds for years exist only in their minds, and nowhere else. And once exposed for what it is, delusion no longer has the power to delude.

My point is that the teachings themselves, *as we have them now*, if applied with skill and perseverance, can help people with the kind of problems we actually face today.

Let's take one final example: how inspiring and healing it can be for a person who suffers from a lack of love, who sees themselves stuck in a history of pain, or who feels they have never been loved, to discover how to receive the love and blessings of the buddhas, through the teachings themselves. It can hand them a new way of looking at themselves and teach them that there is an inexhaustible treasure of love and compassion locked inside them, waiting only for their heart to open in order to be free. Entering the love and compassion of the teachings reveals a well of love within, from which a person can then draw to give to others.

INTEGRATION

Then again, what is so important for the teachings and practice to have their full impact, yet is often neglected, is *integration.* For the Dharma to strengthen itself for the future, and for individuals to survive and accomplish something on the spiritual path, we must examine deeply how a student can be helped through the different stages of the path, described by Milarepa's disciple Gampopa in his famous prayer:

Grant your blessings so that my mind may turn
    towards the Dharma
Grant your blessings so that Dharma may progress
    along the path
Grant your blessings so that the path may clarify
    confusion
Grant your blessings so that confusion may dawn as
    wisdom.

All too often, people will enter the Dharma, but somehow just wait passively for the teachings to come to them. We need to be more active in engaging with the teachings, applying them to ourselves and making a conscious effort to keep them alive. We may hear the teachings, but how little we put them into action! That's why we need to hear them again and again, so that what we should do becomes so clear that it is almost second nature. Then, through practice, it becomes a natural good habit. Otherwise there's a huge gulf between what we aspire to and what we are, and our spiritual aspirations leave us behind.

Frequently we resist change and embed ourselves in samsara, letting the truth of the teachings waft over us like a breeze, touching us only superficially. We somehow fend off the truth of the teachings by rationalising them, reducing them to the ordinary, or 'spiritualising' them, rather than taking them personally.

Our greatest problem, without any doubt, is the way we forget. Forgetting is ignoring, and ignoring is ignorance. One moment we can realise something earth-shattering, and be incredibly inspired, and then in the next, what with distraction, ego and samsara, it's gone. Many teachers must sometimes feel a little like Avalokiteshvara, who, after having saved innumerable beings from the hell-realms, was grief-stricken to look back and see that countless more were pouring in.

So whatever realisation or understanding we have, we must let it have its full impact; only this will allow it to bring transformation. Realisation is one thing, but following it and living up to it is quite another. By constantly recalling and adding up our moments of realisation, even recording them in a book of insights, we will find that they will validate the teachings, and make them more and more powerful. Students need to make their realisations vivid, take care of them and apply the teachings, so they do not fall back into their old habits.

In a way, any realisation is a commitment: to the teachings, the teacher and ourselves. There is a responsibility, in fact, on the part of the student towards the teachings: to remember them, to apply them to themselves again and again, and to sustain their clarity.

A discipline like this becomes a training of the mind: slowly, obscurations are broken down, and increasingly we see that negative emotions are only as real as we make them. Occupying the mind with the practice and the teaching gradually leaves less room for the emotions to creep in and sweep us away.

I feel very strongly that there is something here of great importance to the future of the Buddhadharma in the West.

When there are so many ways in which people can get stuck on the path, or become distracted, or abandon it altogether, what kind of support can they find? In the words of His Holiness the Dalai Lama: 'In the East, even if you don't want to practise, the culture draws you in; in the West if you do want to practise, the culture pulls you back.' There is no existing spiritual culture in most parts of the modern world, and everything is geared towards discouraging spiritual practice rather than encouraging it. A correspondingly vigorous effort is needed to help people not only survive, but accomplish their practice and enhance it.

So in a deep sense, integration is itself the future, because when we immerse ourselves in the teaching and practice, we are safeguarding the Dharma, in ourselves. And out of that will come all kinds of appropriate actions. Thich Nhat Hanh said: 'Engaged Buddhism does not only mean to use Buddhism to solve social and political problems. First of all, we have to bring Buddhism into our daily lives.'

The Support of the Sangha

A factor of vital and increasing significance for the
future is the Sangha and the support that it can give,
through real communication, with genuine spiritual
friends. Research (like that of Dr Dean Ornish in his
Love and Survival) has shown how love and emotional
support have a direct effect on physical health and the
length of someone's life. The same will hold true for a
Sangha in which practitioners are supportive of one
another: it will have a deeply positive, healing and
protective effect on the individual members, and on the
ability of the community to sustain itself. The strength
of the Sangha is particularly important in the West,
where there is no culture to support Dharma values.

I have seen how often, with pure love and sincere
friendship, people can be supported through all kinds
of upheavals and challenges. When we fall prey to
misunderstandings and confusion, when emotions flare
up and are blown out of all proportion by
circumstances, we need help, and to be pointed towards
the right teachings. Without any judgement, but with
understanding and complete acceptance, a spiritual
friend can show and remind someone of the Dharma,
always bringing them back to the path with skill and
sensitivity. In the same way it can be immensely
encouraging and supportive when students share their
experience with one another.

The essence of the Buddhadharma is about
individual transformation, and the future lies in

individuals who embody and carry the Dharma, more than in great institutions. The main question for the future of the teaching in the modern world is how those who are following the teachings can be helped and inspired to find the right *inner and outer environment* in which to practise them fullly, follow them through and come to realise and embody their heart essence.

Creating environments where people can come to train deeply in the Buddhadharma underlines the place of communities, and their importance for the future of Buddhism in the West: communities of individuals, wherever they may be, in the city or the countryside, practising and learning together over long periods of time.

The importance of real monastic centres is beyond question. But what kind of environment do we create for ordained men and women? If a nourishing environment is created, with real support, then it's easier for monks and nuns to live as monks and nuns. They need that emotional support, too. Just an institution on its own is sometimes not enough.

As the majority of the students in the West are lay people, so we also need to explore a middle way between monastic life and ordination and ordinary lay practitioners. That is why, in our community, we have developed what we call a 'practising Sangha': these are students who dedicate themselves to practice, and who usually live in a centre, where they divide their day between a regular schedule of practice, work and receiving teachings.

Another important issue is how to help those who don't have a Sangha close to where they live. Here, we have to have a long-term vision and, if possible, options of courses of varying levels and duration. We need to find ways whereby in the absence of a nearby Sangha, people can become a friend to themselves, and create a Dharma environment in their own home, with the aid of the teachings, and with materials like audio tapes, videos, books and manuals. Periodically they should meet the nearest Sangha community, clarify their practice, choose a Dharma brother or sister with whom they feel a special link and whom they can call, and, from time to time, they should attend a major teaching or retreat. By being creative with different elements such as these, an individual can really be helped to follow the path and overcome challenges and difficulties. This is what we have been seeking to develop in our communities.

Conclusion

So, openness between the different traditions; maintaining the purity of the lineage; patience, understanding and skilful means when it comes to change; the training of students and teachers; the completeness of study and practice; a deeper appreciation, application and integration of the teachings; the support of the Sangha and the growth of communities and Dharma environments – all of these have their part to play in securing the future of the Buddhadharma.

Buddhism has reached a point where, certainly as regards the Tibetan tradition, each lineage should look into its own future and hold meaningful conferences or councils with leading masters, just as happened in Samye in Tibet in the eighth century.

Also I cannot agree more that *education* must be our priority, to provide different kinds of trainings – on the one hand a traditional Buddhist training in scriptural study and practice, but directed towards modern people, and on the other hand trainings for those who will not follow with the same intensity, or aimed at specific sectors of the community or interests. I concur fully with my old friend Bob Thurman on our need to offer the heart of Buddhism to the education system at every level, and to create contemplative universities.

The future of humanity is linked to the accessibility of spiritual teachings like the Buddhadharma. This is clear by any analysis, and it is the practicality and ingenuity of the West that can make the Dharma more accessible. In countries such as America there is an almost desperate hunger and need for spiritual vision. I feel that the Buddhadharma can play a great part in answering this need for all kinds of people, and in building a spiritual culture here in the West.

The Dalai Lama has said: 'A new way of thinking has become the necessary condition for responsible living and acting. If we maintain obsolete values and beliefs, a fragmented consciousness and a self-centred spirit, we will continue to hold to outdated goals and behaviours.' With its radical outlook on the world, its treasures like its training in compassion and its knowledge of interdependence, the Buddhadharma *is* handing us a new way of thinking, and more. And – as always – it addresses directly the issues of our time.

Dedication:

Finally, I'd like to pray: for the long life of the teachers, East and West; that the teachings of Buddha continue to thrive here in the West; that all of you progress swiftly along the path to buddhahood; and that all beings be free from suffering and attain the ultimate happiness of enlightenment. Let me also add my appreciation and gratitude to Al Rapaport, for his vision and hard work in imagining and putting together the Buddhism in America conferences.

2

The Spiritual Heart of Tibetan Medicine:

Its Contribution to the Modern World

Your Holiness, eminent doctors and scholars, ladies and gentlemen, it is a great honour for me to address you today at this International Congress of Tibetan Medicine. What I shall endeavour to do is to explore, very briefly and with my limited understanding, the spiritual and mental dimensions of healing within the Buddhist tradition of Tibet. I will speak from my own experience of what I know to be effective in the West. Of course, whatever I do understand is only thanks to the infinite kindness of my masters, and especially Jamyang Khyentse Chökyi Lodrö, Dudjom Rinpoche and Dilgo Khyentse Rinpoche, who embody so perfectly the wisdom and compassion of the Buddhist path.

The ancient science of Tibetan medicine is rooted in the teachings of Buddha, and the essence of these teachings is the central importance of the mind. The Buddha said:

"Commit not a single unwholesome action,
   Cultivate a wealth of virtue,

To tame this mind of ours –
This is the teaching of the Buddha."

He also said:

"We are what we think.
All that we are
Arises with our thoughts.
With our thoughts we make the world.
Speak or act with a pure mind –
And happiness will follow you." [1]

The mind is both the source of happiness and the root of suffering: at the same time as it possesses an extraordinary capacity for healing, it also plays its part in making us ill.

But how exactly can the mind provoke physical illness? The Four Tantras, the authoritative sources for Tibetan medicine, are quite explicit:

Here is an explanation of the *general* cause of all illness. There is but one single cause ... and this is said to be ignorance due to not understanding the meaning of 'selflessness' ...

Now for the *specific* causes: from ignorance arise the three *poisons* of attachment, hatred and closed-mindedness, and from these, as a result, are produced disorders of wind, bile and phlegm.[2]

The basic source of sickness is diagnosed as 'ignorance', in other words attributing a false sense of a lasting and independent self to ourselves and the phenomena around us. This, the Tibetan medical tradition tells us, arouses:

✿ craving and desire that are responsible for disorders of the 'wind';
✿ hatred and pride causing disorders of the 'bile';
✿ and bewilderment and closed-mindedness provoking ailments of the 'phlegm'.

For years now around the world there has been a growing understanding of the correlation of mind and body, and of the link between ill-health and the way we cope with stress and our emotions. In his book *Emotional Intelligence*, Daniel Goleman writes:

People who experienced chronic anxiety, long periods of sadness and pessimism, unremitting tension or incessant hostility, relentless cynicism or suspiciousness, were found to have *double* the risk of disease … . This order of magnitude makes distressing emotions as *toxic* a risk factor as, say, smoking or high cholesterol are for heart disease – in other words, a major threat to health.'[3]

Just as distressing states of mind can cause disorders, so positive, uplifting states can promote good health: states such as peace of mind, optimism, confidence, humour, companionship, joy, love, kindness, compassion and devotion. Again, this has also been observed countless times in the West, and more recently, for example, with Norman Cousins, who laughed his way back to health, and the findings of Dr Dean Ornish, published in his *Love and Survival,* on the effects of emotional support and love on physical health and life expectancy.[4]

Training the Mind

The whole thrust of Buddhist practice is, precisely, to eliminate these negative states of mind and cultivate the positive ones, so transforming our mind and its emotions and thereby healing our entire being: body, speech, mind and heart.

The Buddhist approach to transforming the mind begins by working with our *attitudes* to life, using the power of reason to analyse our delusions, disturbing emotions and even basic assumptions so as to find, simply speaking, a way of being happy. Tibetan master Dodrupchen Jikmé Tenpé Nyima spells out the link between peace of mind, happiness and health:

Whenever you are harmed by sentient beings, or anything else, if you make a habit out of just perceiving only the suffering, then when even the smallest problem comes up, it will cause you enormous anguish in your mind. This is because the nature of any perception or idea, be it happiness or sorrow, is to grow stronger and stronger by being repeated. When the power of this repetitive experience gradually increases, after a while most of what you perceive will become the cause of actually attracting unhappiness towards you, and *happiness will never get a chance ...*

When you are *not* at the mercy of the suffering caused by anxiety, then not only will all other kinds of suffering evaporate like weapons dropping from the hands of soldiers, but even illnesses will normally disappear on their own.

The saints of the past used to say: 'When you are not unhappy, or discontent about anything, then the mind will not be disturbed. If the mind is not disturbed, the inner air (wind) will not be disturbed. That means the other elements of the body will not be disturbed either. Because of this your mind will remain undisturbed, and *the wheel of constant happiness* will turn.[5]

Such a contemplation forms part of the Buddhist Training of the Mind in loving kindness and compassion, which is called *lojong*. When the ultimate cause of all our suffering and sickness is our holding on to a false view of self, our constant selfish grasping and the negative emotions it provokes, then nothing could be more effective or skilful as a remedy than to steep the mind in love, compassion, altruism and thinking of others.

The Buddhist practices of compassion and love are immensely powerful at transforming the emotions, and healing ourselves and others, and one which has had an enormous impact among Western people is *tonglen*, the practice of 'giving and taking'. In their imagination, the practitioner summons all their resources of positive emotion, and trains in taking (through compassion) the suffering and illnesses of others and giving (with love) every source and kind of happiness and well-being.

Tonglen practice reduces and eliminates the grasping ego, while enhancing our concern for others. As a result, what has been discovered is that it is *deeply* therapeutic, especially for those who feel in their lives the sense of lack or unfulfilment or even 'self-hate' which are so prevalent these days. This is why I have developed a series of practices applying tonglen, in order to help bring about such healing.

In Tibet, the healing power of tonglen was legendary; in the West today, the potential of such practices is largely unexplored, but they could, I believe, have astounding results if applied more widely in cases of mental and physical illness.

Meditation

The other practice I would like to mention, one which so many who are working with the sick have, in one context or another, found to be a profound source of healing, is meditation. The spirit of Buddhist meditation is captured so beautifully by Nyoshul Khen Rinpoche:

"Rest in natural great peace
This exhausted mind
Beaten helpless by karma and neurotic thought,
Like the relentless fury of the pounding waves
In the infinite ocean of samsara.
Rest in Natural Great Peace."[6]

Through the practice of 'calm abiding', or tranquillity meditation, our restless, thinking mind subsides into a state of deep inner peace. The warring, fragmented aspects of ourselves begin to settle and become friends; negativity and aggression are disarmed; frustration, tension and turbulent emotions are defused; and the unkindness and harm in us is removed, revealing our inherent 'Good Heart'. So meditation is real *inner disarmament*.

From this state of 'calm abiding' comes the expansive clarity and insight of 'clear seeing': duality dissolves; ego dwindles and confusion evaporates; the whole way we look at ourselves changes; and we give space to emotions, learn from them, and become free from their sway.

As this 'clear seeing' progressively deepens, it leads us to an experience of the intrinsic nature of reality, and the nature of our mind. For when the cloud-like thoughts and emotions fade away, the sky-like nature of our true being is revealed and, shining from it, our buddha nature – bodhicitta – like the sun. And just as both light and warmth blaze from the sun, wisdom and loving compassion radiate from the mind's innermost nature. Grasping at a false self or ego has dissolved, and we simply rest, inasmuch as we can, in the nature of mind, this most natural state which is without any reference or concept, hope or fear, yet with a quiet but soaring confidence – the deepest form of well-being imaginable.

One oral instruction from the great masters of the past, for me, resonates this innermost nature of mind:

Chu ma nyok na dang
Sem ma cho na de

Nothing could be simpler, yet more powerful: water, if unstirred, will become clear – that's a fact. In just the same way, the very nature of mind is such that if you do not alter, fabricate, or manipulate it with needless thinking, it will, by itself, find its own natural state of peace and well-being.

So many have found that even a glimpse of the nature of mind is utterly transforming, nourishing, and purifying. For if dis-ease is due to our losing sight of our true nature, to recognise the nature of our mind must be the ultimate healing.

Padmasambhava, who introduced Buddhism into Tibet in the eighth century, clarifies this even further:

Don't regard illness as a hindrance, or consider it a virtue. Leave your mind unfabricated and free ... cutting through the flow of conceptual thoughts ... old illnesses will disappear by themselves and you remain unharmed by new ones.

Conclusion

Healing practices generally fall into three different approaches: prevention; applying antidotes or transformation. They could be compared, to take an everyday example, to avoiding your enemy, confronting and dealing with him, or turning him into a friend. I have touched only on meditation and on training the mind in loving kindness and compassion, but there is a vast range of healing practices, especially within the Vajrayana Buddhist tradition where healing is achieved through transformation. They employ every kind of skilful means – visualisation, mental imagery, sound, mantra, movement and yoga – and embrace every facet of the human mind – imagination, intellect and emotion. A number of these methods have been used to great effect to help combat illnesses such as cancer and AIDS.

Finally, the real power and strength of the lineage of Tibetan Buddhism is, I feel, seen most clearly in its great practitioners and masters, whose mere presence is deeply healing in itself. It is our good fortune to live in the same era as one such person – His Holiness the Dalai Lama.

It is largely due to His Holiness, I believe, that Tibetan medicine has endured and thrived in the way that it has; I would like to salute here the Tibetan Medical and Astrological Institute in Dharamsala in India, which was one of the very first Tibetan institutions to have been established by His Holiness in exile. At the same time, let me also pay tribute to all the other Tibetan physicians and centres of Tibetan medicine around the world.

To see a major conference like this on Tibetan Medicine, attended by so many eminent doctors, scientists and scholars from all over the globe, gives me enormous pleasure; I applaud it and congratulate the organisers with all my heart. It presents us with an exciting opportunity, and I hope that in the wake of this Congress, the dialogue will continue. The holistic approach of Tibetan medicine, which deals with both mind and body, holds tremendous promise, but so far we have only skimmed the surface of what it has to offer the world. As we enter the twenty-first century we can and should imagine research of many kinds, for example into how to make these amazing Buddhist healing methods available alongside Tibetan medicine, in the right environment and to patients who would be receptive, and so explore their combined power of healing.

And yet, in order for the Tibetan medical tradition to be more effective in serving people's needs, two things are required: (1) a greater understanding and communication among Tibetan doctors themselves, and (2) closer collaboration between Tibetan physicians and Western doctors and scientists, though this must never compromise the integrity of Tibetan Medicine. For, as His Holiness says:

> Tibetan medicine is an integrated system of health care that has served the Tibetan people well for many centuries and which, I believe, can still provide much benefit to humanity at large. The difficulty we face in bringing this about is one of communication, for like other scientific systems, Tibetan medicine must be understood in its own terms, as well as in the context of objective investigation.[7]

Once these conditions have been realised, Tibetan medicine will take its rightful place as a universally respected, major system of medicine and healing, and prove itself to have more and more to offer, in a world increasingly beset with diseases and disorders, towards relieving suffering everywhere.

3

View and Wrong View

The Buddha once told a story about a young man who was a trader and had a beautiful wife and baby son. Sadly, his wife fell ill and died and the man poured all his love into his little child, who became the sole source of his happiness and joy. Once while he went away on business, bandits raided his village, burned it to the ground and captured his five-year-old son. When he returned and saw the devastation, he was beside himself with grief. He found the charred corpse of a small child and, in his desperation, took it for the body of his son. He tore at his hair and beat his chest and wept uncontrollably. At last, he arranged a cremation ceremony, collected up the ashes, and put them in a very precious silk pouch. Whether he was working, sleeping or eating, he always carried that bag of ashes with him, and often he would sit alone and weep, for hours on end.

One day his son escaped from the bandits and found his way home. It was midnight when he arrived at his father's new house and knocked on the door. The man lay in bed, sobbing, the bag of ashes by his side. 'Who is it?' he asked. The child answered, 'It's me, Daddy, it's your son. Open the door.' In his anguish and confusion, all that the father could think of was that some malicious boy was playing a cruel trick on him. 'Go away,' he shouted, 'leave me alone.' Then he started to cry once more. Again and again, the boy knocked, but the father refused to let him in. Finally, he slowly turned and walked away. The father and son never saw one another again.

When he came to the end of his story, the Buddha said, 'Sometime, somewhere you take something to be the truth. But if you cling to it too strongly, then even when the truth comes in person and knocks on your door, you will not open it.'

What is it that makes us cling so strongly to our assumptions and beliefs, so strongly that we miss the truth and ignore reality altogether, like the father in the Buddha's story? In the Buddhist teachings, we speak of 'one ground and two paths'. By this we mean that, even though the 'ground' of our original nature is the same, the buddhas recognise their true nature, become enlightened and take one 'path'; we do not recognise, become confused, and take another. In that failure to recognise, that wasteland of unawareness, we invent and construct a reality all of our own. We make what is in fact a wrong view into our view, the view that shapes our whole lives and colours our perception of everything. Wrong views, according to the Buddha, are the worst, and the source, of all those harmful actions of our body, speech and mind that trap us endlessly in the cycle of suffering known as samsara.

In his very first teaching, the Buddha explained that the root cause of suffering is ignorance. But where exactly is this ignorance? And how does it display itself? Let's take an everyday example. We all know someone who is gifted with an intelligence that is remarkably powerful and sophisticated. Isn't it puzzling how, instead of helping them, as you might expect, it only seems to make them suffer even more? It is almost as if their brilliance is in fact directly responsible for their pain.

What is happening is quite clear: this intelligence of ours is captured and held hostage by ignorance, which then makes use of it freely for its own ends. This is how we can be extraordinarily intelligent and yet absolutely wrong at one and the same time. This is how we can find such certainty in taking something wrong as right, and yet go through the most appalling suffering, often without even realising it. Surely one of the most heart-breaking aspects of our lives is that we cannot recognise the fundamental cause of our suffering. Isn't it curious how we cannot detect ignorance at work? But, you see, this lack of awareness is exactly what ignorance, *ma rigpa* in Tibetan, is.

There could be no bigger mistake than to think that ignorance is somehow dumb and stupid, or passive and lacking in intelligence. On the contrary, it is shrewd and cunning, versatile and ingenious in the games of deception, and in our wrong views and their burning convictions we find one of its deepest and, as Buddha said, most dangerous, manifestations:

What do you have to fear from the wild elephant
Who can only damage your body here and now,
When falling under the influence of misguided
    people and wrong views
Not only destroys the merit you have accumulated
    in the past,
But also blocks your path to freedom in the future?

Using our intelligence, then, we fortify our wrong view
and construct around us a carefully tended,
impregnable defence system. Once we have doubts,
then everywhere we find allies to help us doubt. We
raise a protective dome of doubt about us, which must
at all costs be tight and seamless, with no fatal cracks to
let understanding filter through.

Wrong views and wrong convictions can be the most
devastating of all our delusions. Surely both Adolf
Hitler and Pol Pot must have been convinced that they
were right? And yet each and every one of us has that
same dangerous tendency as they had: to form
convictions, believe them without question and act on
them, so bringing down suffering not only on ourselves,
but also on all those around us.

    On the other hand, the heart of Buddha's teaching is
to see 'the actual state of things, as they are', and this is
called the true View. It is a view which is all-embracing,
as the role of spiritual teachings is precisely to give us a
complete perspective on the nature of mind and reality.

The teachings are said to have two effects: first, to eliminate ego; second, to give us the wisdom of discernment, to know what is appropriate and just. This is why it is so vital to have a firm grounding in the teachings, for it is only this that will bring a breeze of sanity and wisdom into our confusion, and sweep away the distortion and suffering of wrong views.

Of course, people are different, and for some it will take longer than others truly to hear the teaching, so that it 'clicks' for them somewhere deep in their hearts and minds. But when that happens, then you really have a View. Whatever difficulties you face, you will find you have some kind of serenity, stability and understanding, and an internal mechanism – you could call it an 'inner transformer' – that works for you, to protect you from falling prey to wrong views. In that view, you will have discovered a 'wisdom guide' of your own, always on hand to advise you, support you and remind you of the truth. Confusion will still arise, that's only normal, but with a crucial difference: no longer will you focus on it in a blinkered and obsessive way, but you will look on it with humour, perspective and compassion.

Let's look deeper into wrong views, because the fact is that many people do not have this sturdy grounding in the teachings. And without it, we can be convinced or persuaded, so easily, of almost anything. Once we are wrongly convinced, then we find no end of doubts, distortions and misconceptions to feed our wrong convictions, night and day, to prove how right we are. Whenever we cannot understand something, or we feel in a negative state of mind, we cast around to find reasons to justify our confusion and negativity. Like a demented lawyer, we obsessively marshal our arguments, weighing all the evidence in our favour and suppressing any other explanations, especially the truth.

We find that we only dare mix with and speak to those people who will fuel our false convictions. For although we keep up the appearance of seeming open, we can not allow ourselves to risk being exposed to other points of view, and we are anyway too proud ever to admit that we could have made a mistake. Our memory becomes selective, choosing to recall only the darkness, pain and confusion and erasing anything that is awkwardly uplifting or constructive, or could point towards happiness or truth.

By now, our wrong views and convictions have a power and energy entirely of their own. We can no longer recognise the truth if it stares us in the face or hammers on our door. We are locked into an endless loop of self-destruction, systematically rejecting and destroying anything positive or truly beneficial because it might jeopardise the fragile creation of ignorance and ego. How many of us go through life turning our backs again and again on what may even be the most precious opportunities we will ever know, denying all that is good or helpful, choosing whatever is destructive and harmful and attracting suffering like a magnet? Trapped in a prison of our own design, all we can do is complain that we are impotent and helpless, and put the blame on circumstances or our lives or other people.

Why do such things happen? This is a very complex question; there could be so many reasons. Of course, it might be when a distant memory of some agonising, half-buried childhood experience is triggered in our mind, and that memory mixes and becomes confused with reality. Or it could be for no apparent reason that abruptly we are faced by a seemingly illogical psychological crisis. It can also happen that when we see too much truth about ourselves suddenly mirrored in front of us by the teacher or the teachings, it is simply too difficult to face, too terrifying to recognise, too painful to accept as the reality about ourselves. We deny and reject it, in an absurd and desperate attempt to defend ourselves from ourselves, from the truth of who we really are. And when there are things too powerful or too difficult to accept about ourselves, our arrogance and false pride refuse to let us acknowledge them and we project them on to the world around us, usually on to those who help us and love us the most – our teacher, the teachings, our parents or our closest friend.

How can we possibly penetrate the tough shield of this defensive system? The very best solution is when we can ourselves recognise that we are living duped by our own delusions. I have seen how for many people a glimpse of the truth, the true View, can bring the whole fantastic construction of wrong views, fabricated by ignorance, tumbling instantly to the ground.

Yet this is so very, very difficult. The more we fortify ourselves behind our wrong views, the less chance there is for transformation. We are often so stuck in our minds, in our own little individual worlds of emotional and psychological suffering. We may turn to spirituality or to therapy, but instead of bringing us freedom and purification, they are neutralised, conscripted by ignorance and end up as weapons in our own hands, turned against us. And if we call them 'helpful', it is only because they 'help' us reproduce and prolong our patterns of delusion. They cannot truly help us if somewhere we do not recognise or admit to ourselves that we are going wrong.

As we follow the teachings and as we practise, we will inevitably discover certain truths about ourselves that stand out prominently: there are those places where we always get stuck; there are those habitual patterns and strategies which are the legacy of negative karma and which we continually repeat and reinforce; there are those particular ways of seeing things, those tired old explanations of ourselves and the world around us, which are quite mistaken yet which we hold on to as authentic and so distort our whole view of reality. When we persevere on the spiritual path, and examine ourselves honestly, it begins to dawn on us more and more that our perceptions are nothing more than a web of illusions. Yet simply to acknowledge our confusion, even though we cannot accept it completely, can bring some light of understanding and spark off in us a new process, a process of healing.

Our minds can be wonderful, but at the same time they can be our very worst enemies. They give us so much trouble. Sometimes I wish the mind were like a set of dentures, which we could take out and leave on our bedside table overnight. At least we would get a break from its tiring and tiresome escapades. We are so at the mercy of our minds that even when we find that the teachings strike a chord inside us, and move us more than anything we have ever experienced, still we hold back because of some deep-seated and inexplicable suspicion. Somewhere along the line, though, we have to stop mistrusting. We have to let go of the suspicion and doubt that are supposed to protect us but never work and which only end up hurting us even more than what they are supposed to defend us from.

When we are feeling in a negative frame of mind, it is only natural to doubt rather than to believe. From a Buddhist point of view, doubt is a sign of a lack of a complete understanding, and a lack of spiritual education, but it is also seen as a catalyst in the maturing of faith. It is when we face doubts and difficulties that we discover whether our faith is a simplistic, pious and conceptual one or whether it is strong, enduring and anchored in a deep understanding in the heart. If you have faith, sooner or later it may well be put to the test, and wherever the challenge may come from, from within you or from outside, it is simply part of the process of faith and doubt.

Imagine that you had gone all your life without ever washing and then one day you decide to take a shower. You start scrubbing away, but then watch in horror as the dirt begins to ooze out of the pores of your skin and stream down your body. Something must be wrong: you were supposed to be getting cleaner and all you can see is grime. You panic and fling yourself out of the shower, convinced that you should never have begun. But you only end up even more dirty than before. You have no way of knowing that the wisest thing to do is to be patient and to finish the shower. It may look for a while as if you are getting even dirtier, but if you keep on washing, you will emerge fresh and clean. It's all a process, the process of purification.

So when little obstacles crop up on the spiritual path, a good practitioner does not lose faith and begin to doubt, but has the discernment to recognise difficulties, whatever they may be, for what they are – just obstacles, and nothing more. It is the nature of things that when you recognise an obstacle as such, it ceases to be an obstacle. Equally, it is by failing to recognise an obstacle for what it is, and therefore taking it seriously, that it is empowered and solidified and becomes a real blockage.

Whenever doubt arises, then, see it just as an obstacle, recognise it as an understanding that is calling out to be clarified or unblocked and know that it is not a fundamental problem, but simply a stage in the process of purification and learning. Allow the process to continue and complete itself and never lose your trust or resolve. This is the way followed by all the great practitioners of the past, who used to say 'there is no armour like perseverance'.

The teachings tell us what it is we need to realise, but we also have to go on our own journey in order to come to a personal realisation. That journey may take us through suffering, difficulties and doubts of all kinds, but they will become our greatest teachers. Through them we will learn the humility to recognise our limitations, and through them we will discover the inner strength and fearlessness we need to emerge from our old habits and set patterns, and surrender into the vaster vision of real freedom offered by the spiritual teachings.

So, again and again we need to appreciate the subtle workings of the teaching and the practice and, even when there is no extraordinary, dramatic change, to persevere with calm and patience. How important it is to be skilful and gentle with ourselves, without becoming disheartened or giving up, but trusting the spiritual path and knowing that it has its own laws and its own dynamics.

Then we need, above all else, to nourish our true self – what you could call our buddha nature – for so often we make the fatal mistake of identifying with our confusion and then use it to judge and condemn ourselves, and feed that lack of self-love so many of us suffer from today. How vital it is to refrain from the temptation to judge ourselves or the teachings, but to be humorously aware of our condition, and to realise that we are, at the moment, as if many people all living in one person. And how encouraging it can be to accept that, from one perspective, we all have huge problems which we bring to the spiritual path, and which indeed may have led us to the teachings, and yet to know from another point of view that ultimately our problems are not so real, so solid or so insurmountable as we have told ourselves.

For us to survive on the spiritual path, there are many challenges to face and there is much to learn. We have to discover how to deal with obstacles and difficulties, how to process doubts and see through wrong views, how to inspire ourselves when we least feel like it, how to understand ourselves and our moods, how really to work with and integrate the teachings and practices, how to evoke compassion and enact it in life, and how to transform our suffering and emotions.

On the spiritual path, all of us need the support and the good foundation that come from really knowing the teachings, and this cannot be stressed strongly enough. For the more we study and practise, the more we shall embody discernment, clarity and insight. Then, when the truth comes knocking, we will know it with certainty for what it is, and gladly open the door, because we'll have guessed that it may well be the truth of who we really are.

(This article was first published in View, *Summer 1994.)*

4

Misunderstandings

I remember a story I first heard when I was a child growing up in Tibet. It comes from the *Jataka Tales*, the accounts of Buddha's previous lives, and tells of the time he was born as a lion who lived on the edge of a deep forest. One autumn day a tremendous commotion broke out and all the animals began to stampede. The lion saw them, in their hundreds and thousands, running for their lives without daring to look behind them. He knew that if they were not stopped they would run as far as the sea and drown. Quickly, he leapt up on to a hill which overlooked their path and roared three times. The animals all stopped at once, one pressed against the next in a huge, trembling mass. The lion walked down from the hill and asked them why they were running so fast.

'The end of the world is coming!' they cried.

'Who said so?' asked the lion.

'The elephants,' they said.

'No it wasn't,' said the elephants indignantly, 'it was the lions.'

'No, it was the tigers who told us,' said the lions.

The tigers said it was the rhinos; the rhinos said it was

the buffaloes; the buffaloes said it was the antelopes; the antelopes said it was the gazelles; and the gazelles said it was the rabbits.

The rabbits said: 'It was this little rabbit here who told us!'

The lion strode over to the little rabbit and asked, 'How do you know it's the end of the world?'

'I heard it, sir, a terrible cracking noise, and I saw something out of the corner of my eye.'

'Where?' said the lion. 'Tell me exactly what happened.'

'I was sitting under a fruit tree, thinking about what would become of me when the end of the world came, and all of a sudden I heard this cracking noise ... as if the earth itself was splitting apart.'

'Let's go and have a look,' said the lion, and the rabbit climbed on his back and showed him the way. When they got near his tree, the rabbit jumped off, because he was too scared to go near the crack in the earth. The lion went up to the tree and saw where the rabbit had been sitting, and he saw the fruit which had fallen and crackled as it crushed the autumn leaves. He called the rabbit and showed him, and then they told the animals that their terror had all been for no reason whatsoever. And that it was not the end of the world. So often we make something huge out of a simple problem, and blow it out of all proportion. How many of our difficulties start with one tiny misunderstanding: someone didn't give us their usual smile today; our teacher gave us a stern look or our best friend criticised us; this morning's cup of coffee tasted bitter; we woke up feeling a bit cranky ... that's all it takes to ruin our whole day! We can find ourselves so fragile, so insecure, so frail and vulnerable that any off-hand remark, any hasty reaction or ill-timed joke can puncture our confidence completely. If we don't catch the misunderstanding there and then, it can act like a seed that germinates and grows bigger and bigger. Small problems fester and expand into enormous fears and emotional earthquakes, and no matter how minute our suffering might be in truth, we imagine, like the rabbit, that it's the end of the world.

Of course, we may not be able to pinpoint exactly what's wrong – it might only be a slightly bad mood – but somewhere we want to make the most out of it. We revel in self-pity or depression. But above all, we cannot let go of it. As if hell-bent on bringing everything to a painful point, almost as if we wanted to take revenge on someone or something – which always turns out to be ourselves – we lurch unfailingly towards a crisis. Meanwhile our delusion, or our depression, looms like some macabre sculpture we are fashioning, or a building we are feverishly constructing, enlarging and extending, and finally topping with the discovery of some deep-seated, ancient problem, so that everything is assembled into an ideal home, complete with all the best reasons why we should be depressed. Yet what escapes us all along, apart from the fact that our problem is not even that serious, let alone disastrous, is this: it is all built from nothing! It does not really exist.

In the summer of 1900 the Tibetan mystic Tertön Sogyal began to reveal a cycle of teachings and meditation practices which had been hidden more than a thousand years earlier by the extraordinary master Padmasambhava. At the heart of his revelation is a remarkable instruction on transforming faults in the system of interdependence that governs all our lives. I was amazed when I first read its opening lines:

> The root of all faults, all failings, is nothing other than ignorance. This ignorance is like mistaking a heap of stones on the horizon for a human figure; it has no basis whatsoever, which means that even the source of these faults and failings does not exist.

Our problems, in other words, all come from nothing; they are all based on a misunderstanding that does not even exist. The more I think about what Padmasambhava said, the more I realise how true it is. With all our ideas, with all our misunderstandings, how often do we ever grasp more than a partial and distorted version of how things really are? Our whole vision of reality in fact amounts to a fabrication, an exaggeration, a fantastic edifice of delusion. Once we miss understanding, we create something based on that missing of the point, which cannot but be a lie and an illusion. And in turn, we swallow the lie and fall for the illusion and take it to be true, like the fool who spends his life chasing after the fabled crock of gold that is buried at the end of a rainbow.

How tragic this all is! For misunderstanding brings with it endless complications: hope and fear, despair and even suicide. We make ourselves suffer, and we create problems for ourselves which are absolutely unnecessary. It's that simple – all we have to do is realise it. And when you do eventually see the truth of just how unnecessary it is, your heart wants to burst with compassion for anyone who is suffering in this way. And yet at the same time you begin to appreciate the absurdity of it all – it's as ridiculous, the Tibetan saying goes, as trying to fix a string on to an egg.

Why on earth do we go through all this – for nothing? It's so difficult for us to see the truth for what it really is because the whole thing is so personalised – we fail to see any other perspective, or notice how much our mind exaggerates. This is one of the symptoms of samsara, the uncontrolled cycle of life and death that we subscribe to. If we only examine them, all these appearances, all these perceptions of ours we take to be so real, are revealed to be completely non-existent. We only need a glimpse of the innermost nature of the mind to see this fake reality for what it is, a way of sabotaging and undermining our true nature, and to see that all our hopes and expectations and fears are the agents of samsara, employed to drain and weaken us.

Even though we may listen to spiritual teachings, and hear the truth again and again that everything is like an illusion, and the delusory appearances of the mind, yet when ignorance is at play it employs such sophisticated or enthralling disguises that we fail to recognise or see it for what it really is. That's what makes us truly 'ignorant'. What I have increasingly come to realise is that when we follow a spiritual path it becomes more important than ever to see through the mind and its delusions, and to know the extent to which misunderstandings dominate our lives. For a spiritual practitioner, it is crucial to be on top of things.

To be on top of things can be taken in many contexts, one of which is that we need to recognise the root of our problems. We know that it's often when someone begins to recognise their fundamental blockage that their healing will begin. But to identify the source of our difficulties and confusion can seem to be so hard and take so long. They are well supported on all sides, and even though we may occasionally have a brief glimpse of the reality of our situation, it's as if everything around us is conspiring to prevent us from being able to see. For it to become clear in our minds may require a particular set of circumstances, or a special environment, or simply a lapse of time. It can also be that the root of our problems lies obscured by our karma, which makes it impossible for us to see what is blocking us, or even for the teacher or a friend to point it out to us clearly. Until that karma is purified, we are not ready to realise what it is. Or perhaps our stubborn pride simply refuses to realise, preferring to take our misunderstanding as the truth, and clinging on to it in devoted attachment because we cannot face our secret suspicions that we are wrong. So many factors come into play, and whether we are able to see clearly into ourselves or not is all to do with the complex workings of inter–dependence.

Everything comes into being because of inter-dependence. When circumstances all fall into place, we call it 'auspicious', and everything fits and unfolds harmoniously. But when something does not quite 'click' then a gap, a vacuum, opens up, and in that absence of clarity misunderstanding creeps in. Once enough inauspicious and rogue ingredients have amassed, they somehow constitute the perfect circumstance needed to prove to us that our misunderstanding is the truth. This allows it to be exploited by others, whatever their motivation, and excites us into making the whole situation more volatile – something inside us almost relishes the drama of it all.

Issues begin to build up, because when we are unclear, we heap everything we are not clear about – all our pain and suffering, all our insecurity, fears, emotions and obsessions – on to our one area of obscurity. So, when we cannot see or we refuse to face our main problem honestly, it will get transferred and bounce around, fastening on to one aspect of our mind and life or another. As soon as one issue is resolved, it will shift to another, and then the next, and so become a recurrent calamity.

Yet if we have an openness and willingness to identify the root of our greatest personal difficulty, and see it clearly for what it is, we may be surprised to find it is not such a gigantic problem. All it may need is a subtle shift. To glimpse the nature of mind, for example, requires only the slightest shift, a different way of looking: of looking into the mind.

The Buddhist scriptures have their own favourite example. Imagine, they say, you were out walking one evening at dusk. Suddenly on the path in front of you, you see what seems to be a snake. You are transfixed with fear; you begin to sweat; your heart pounds and your mind races for some way of escaping the snake, and death. An impulse tells you to switch on your torch, and to your amazement and relief you see that your snake is only a piece of mottled rope. You sigh and cackle nervously. But where was the snake? It was a complete illusion, existing only in your mind, in its concepts and in your habitual tendency to fear, at that instant triggered by misunderstanding and projected immediately on to the harmless length of rope.

Haven't we all, at one time or another, known moments of sudden realisation like this, when all our preconceived ideas about something shifted and betrayed a completely different, sometimes surprising, but always more authentic perspective on reality? Moments like these we should never overlook, because it is in them that we can, in a flash, see samsara, the vicious cycle in which we waste our lives away, revealed as a colossal fabrication, nothing but ignorance, itself non-existent, constructed into a tortuous labyrinth of delusion. Suddenly we realise something, something deep and liberating, about how mind works and how misunderstandings materialise. The trick then is to keep that realisation so that the next time a similar situation arises it will at least be less intense. One thing we can be sure of: if we do not make a point of keeping alive the memory of what we have realised, in no time at all the mind will have found a way to work it off.

Being on top of things also means being able to recognise, and to remember, those special moments when some powerful insight arises and briefly blossoms: a moment of clarity and awakening, when suddenly something becomes strikingly clear; a moment of liberation when the words of a spiritual teaching make things click, carry an understanding we had far deeper and unlock the mystery of integrating spiritual vision with life.

In the Dzogchen teachings, we speak of dissolving everything, in the state of meditation, into the primordial purity of natural simplicity. You will notice moments when everything becomes transparent and you can actually see that natural simplicity is truly how things are. How ridiculous it seems then to stake our happiness and let our confidence hang on some casual, trivial event. Even though the insecurity we experience from a cross word or a severe look in no way affects the real 'us', because we take it too personally it obscures our judgement and weakens our confidence in ourselves. During moments of clarity, however, we can see that the most important thing for us is to come back to ourselves, to recognise what our true nature is, to have confidence in it and to stabilise that confidence till it becomes unshakeable.

Cast your mind back now and re-visualise one such moment: you may have written it down, or it is there in the recesses of your memory. Capture the highlights, the peak experiences, and gather those moments together for yourself, for it is vital that you never lose them or let them go to waste. Why? Because however clear those experiences are in the setting in which they happened, when you change that environment they will fade away. The everyday reality of our ordinary existence is simply too strong; samsara has its own environment, its own support, its community and protectors and influence. They are so powerful and well established, and the resulting negativity offers such seductive and persuasive arguments, that unless you make a determined effort it will be difficult to maintain your inspiration on the spiritual path.

One of my students told me recently that for him to be on top of things meant 'not getting stuck in our old habits'. But how do we avoid getting stuck? By taking the way out, the path which is there, mapped out for us to travel. Don't forget, I said to him, the Buddha's first teaching on the four noble truths, which tells us that there is an end to suffering and a path that leads to the end of suffering. Buddha actually shows us the way out, and if there is anything at all we need to recognise, it is this. Refuse by all means to get stuck in your habits, but go one step further, and follow the path to break out of them.

Friends and students of mine often tell me how they are plagued by some repetitive pattern: their partners keep leaving them; or there is always a problem at work; or again and again they fall out with people. If that keeps happening to you, maybe you need to look at the reason why. But don't make a big deal out of it, or succumb to the mistake we often make of dwelling on our habitual patterns. By thinking 'I'm always doing this ... repeating the same old pattern ... This is what I'm like ... That's just the kind of person I'm always going to be ... I'm doomed ...', all we are doing is empowering and steadily giving a false reality to that which we want to be free from. We will never be able to change if we endlessly play the same old scratched record. Instead, just ask a simple 'Why?'

Whatever the reason may be, and it could turn out to be something unexpectedly simple, you need to identify it, and then you can do something about it. If you continue to feed your problem there is no limit to how inflated it can become, and the whole issue will turn into a fog of complication. You will then be left at the mercy of the only explanations you can still catch sight of, theories of all kinds about who's to blame: your childhood, your father, your mother, your brother, your sister, Buddha, Jesus or God. It's too complicated by far.

So don't keep looking for patterns and tormenting yourself with what's wrong with you: that could be just another pattern. And whatever you do, don't identify yourself with your pain, your suffering and sore spots, otherwise you'll never be free of them. Don't identify with the mistakes you have made, or let yourself believe that simply because you went wrong, you are fundamentally bad or that's all that you are or could ever be. Much more important is to strengthen the good aspects of yourself, to realise and remember what happens in those wonderful moments when you are confident in your nature, when you feel so good that it's almost as if there is no ego, as if all sense of 'self' had completely dissolved, revealing the real you, and there is only compassion, generosity and fearlessness.

In our heart of hearts we all want to make progress, to change, to become enlightened. But we don't need to wait for the perfect situation, for everything to be right, before we can let go and change. We can begin right now. Let's face it, we have no choice but to change – and that lack of choice is a blessing in disguise, for it hands us continuously the opportunity to blossom, to be free of our 'selves' and so to become truly ourselves.

Sometimes, though, we can feel so frustrated at how stuck and resigned we are, and how resistant to change, that we want to alter absolutely everything about ourselves, even our whole appearance. Don't judge yourself or be too ambitious, and don't try to change everything all at once; instead, be sure to change something fundamental. Change has to grow on you, then it's much more stable. Sudden change is like a promise you cannot keep. Keep working slowly and trust that it will work out, because what we discover so often in life is this: when you really let go, whatever you are asking for happens; and when you try for too much, it does not. But letting go does not mean giving up; they are two quite different things. Never give up. But by all means do let go.

This is where the practice of meditation can be so powerful – because it can inspire in us the realisation that we can actually let go, and if we let go, we're free. When we are truly able to let go of some blockage or pattern or obsession, that is the real result of practice; that is the sign that our practice is accomplishing something.

Then everything will prove much easier for us, because we will be so much easier with ourselves. We will discover confidence within: an authentic, natural, indestructible confidence, which will render us fearless. Whatever we have to face, we know we will be able to manage. Our fear, uncertainty and hesitation about whether we can change, or even truly wish to change, are what impel us, for want of any alternative, to put our trust in false refuges, and to sink back into our old, well-worn and familiar patterns of suffering.

Of course, it would be only too easy to sit back and congratulate ourselves on how we had changed, simply to find our subtle patterns easing their way back in, taking a new shape. Because there is no end to the deviousness of our minds, and the wrong views that are ego. We may cut the patterns, but then how do we prevent them from returning? We practise, abiding continuously by the View. The point of practice is to give us a framework, one that works for us, and which recreates a living atmosphere of inspiration, and of the View of the nature of mind.

We often hear about the View, and about having confidence in ourselves, but what do they really mean? What is the mark of whether we have translated the view of the spiritual teachings into our day-to-day existence? It is when we can take the events and upheavals of our lives and let them teach us not only wisdom and discernment, but also means for being skilful, with both others and ourselves.

This is also the mark of whether we are truly on top of things. My students have told me of how they have gone through the hardest moments of their lives, like losing a loved one, when there was no choice but to let go. They said they found that when they let go in the light of their practice and the inspiration of the teachings, gradually over the years, through all the tragedy, through all the letting go, a deep confidence was born. In the unique method of Dzogpachenpo, the masters say that the worse the circumstances, the better it is for you. They do not mean that all the most dreadful catastrophes are queuing up for you as a blessing, but that with your View, you can let go of aversion to harm and difficulties, transforming anything that befalls you into a blessing.

There is a wonderful picture of Buddha which I always remember. He is sitting, unwavering, in meditation in the first watch of the night when he became enlightened. Mara, the embodiment of delusion, ordered his army to attack the Buddha, yet as their weapons came within his radiance, they all transformed from instruments of harm into gifts of adoration, from spears and swords and boiling oil into a rain of soft and fragrant flowers.

(First published as 'Being on Top of Things' in View, *Autumn 1994.)*

Notes

1 From *The Dhammapada*, trans. Thomas Byrom, Vintage, 1996, Chapter 1.

2 See, e.g. *The Quintessence Tantras of Tibetan Medicine*, trans. by Dr Barry Clark, Snow Lion, 1995, pp. 75–6.

3 Daniel Goleman, *Emotional Intelligence*, Bloomsbury, 1996, p.169. Daniel Goleman summarises the data from a number of studies indicating the significance of emotions in medicine.

4 Dean Ornish, *Love and Survival*, HarperCollins, 1996.

5 Dodrupchen Jikmé Tenpé Nyima (1865–1926), *sKyid sDug Lam Khyer*, in his *Collected Works*, Vol. 5, Chorten Gonpa, Gangtok, Sikkim, pp. 351–66. Also translated as 'Instructions on Turning Happiness and Suffering into the Path of Enlightenment' by Tulku Thondup in *Enlightened Living*, Shambhala, 1990, pp. 117–29.

6 Quoted Sogyal Rinpoche, *The Tibetan Book of Living and Dying*, Sogyal Rinpoche, Harper San Francisco, 1992, pp. 62–3.

7 HH the Dalai Lama, foreword to *The Quintessence Tantras of Tibetan Medicine*, trans. by Dr Barry Clark, Snow Lion, 1995.